Lacrosse Warrior

Lacrosse Warrior

Wendy A. Lewis

James Lorimer & Company, Ltd., Publishers
Toronto

James Lorimer & Company Ltd. acknowledges the support of the Ontario Arts Council. We acknowledge the support of the Government of Canada through the Book Publishing Industry Development Program (BPIDP) for our publishing activities. We acknowledge the support of the Canada Council for the Arts for our publishing program. We acknowledge the assistance of the OMDC Book Fund, an initiative of Ontario Media Development Corporation.

Library and Archives Canada Cataloguing in Publication

Lewis, Wendy A., 1966-
    Lacrosse warrior : the life of Mohawk lacrosse champion Gaylord Powless / Wendy Lewis.

(Recordbooks)
ISBN 978-1-55277-002-3 (bound).--ISBN 978-1-55277-001-6 (pbk.)

    1. Powless, Gaylord, 1946-2001--Juvenile literature. 2. Lacrosse players--Canada--Biography--Juvenile literature. 3. Mohawk Indians--Biography--Juvenile literature. I. Title. II. Title: Lacrosse warrior. III. Series.

GV989.L49 2008   j796.34'7092   C2007-907516-9

James Lorimer & Company Ltd., Publishers
317 Adelaide Street West, Suite #1002
Toronto, ON
M5V 1P9
www.lorimer.ca

Distributed in the United States by:
Orca Book Publishers
P.O. Box 468
Custer, WA USA
98240-0468

Printed and bound in Canada

Contents

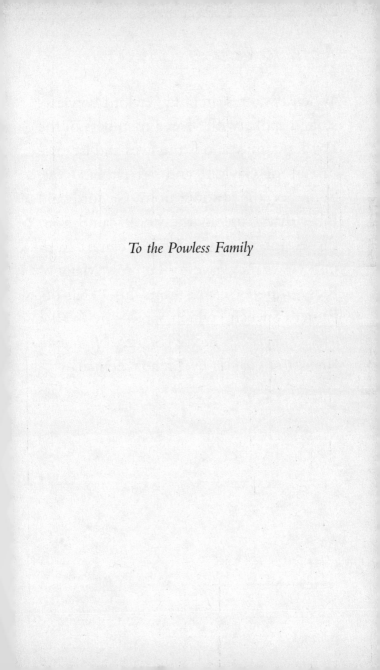

To the Powless Family

Note to Readers

When I was researching Gaylord Powless's story, I spoke with several members of the Powless family about the lives and lacrosse careers of Gaylord and his father, Ross. Some of the quotes from Gaylord and Ross that I use in the book came from those interviews. Others came from interviews they gave to the press. Many of Ross's quotes came from his "Hall-of-Famer's Speech," which appears in *To Run with Longboat: Twelve Stories of Indian Athletes in Canada* by Brenda Zeman.

Prologue

On the arena floor, the players run into position. Two teams. Twelve boys. One ball.

Gaylord Powless crouches for the faceoff. His stomach churns. He's nervous, and wonders why. It's a big game, but they all are to Gaylord. Maybe it's playing in this town that's bothering him. The fans here are tough on Native players. So are the referees. Or maybe he's feeling down because his skin breakouts are bad today. His new nickname at school is "Scabs."

Gaylord tells himself to be happy, not nervous. He's where he loves to be — on the lacrosse floor, stick in his hands. The opposing centre, a brick wall with a mean sneer, crouches down. He spits out an insult that slams Gaylord's Native heritage. Gaylord fights to keep his cool. He knows the centre is trying to make him lose his temper — and the faceoff.

The whistle blows. The boys clash sticks. Gaylord scoops up the ball and charges down the floor. He knows where his teammate will be. They planned this on the bench. He whips the ball into the pocket of his teammate's stick.

WHAM! He gets checked into the boards, hard. Gaylord ignores the pain and races to the shooting line. A teammate throws him the ball. The other team swarms, but it takes just a second for Gaylord to flip the ball into the open corner of the net. He scores!

The cheers of the Six Nations fans are loud and proud. Gaylord's dad won't say much after the game, but Gaylord knows he'll be happy. He always is when Gaylord controls his temper.

The opposing centre shoves past Gaylord. He growls another insult. This time Gaylord grins. He's not nervous anymore. He can play this game. It's one thing he's sure of. He's been playing lacrosse

Gaylord in 1967, practising with his Junior A team, the Green Gaels

since he could walk. His father is Ross Powless, one of the best lacrosse players of all time. This game is in his blood.

The best revenge against players like the centre is to keep cool and play well. That's what Gaylord does. He plays like his dad. He plays like a Powless. He plays like his Mohawk ancestors.

Lacrosse Players from Way Back

Gaylord's Mohawk ancestors moved to Canada from New York State after the American Revolution. They were part of the Iroquois Confederacy, a peaceful union of six nations: the Mohawk, Seneca, Cayuga, Oneida, Onondaga, and Tuscarora nations. For more than 200 years, members of the Powless family have lived, worked, and played lacrosse on the Six Nations of the Grand River Territory near Brantford, Ontario.

1

North America's First Team Sport

Ancient trees tower around the playing field. Quivering in the breeze, they seem as excited as the humans about the Tewaarathon game. Crowds of villagers gather at the tree line. One of the watchers is an old man who is sick. The game is being played for him, to help him get well.

Sixty men file onto the field. They wear loincloths and body paint, and carry webbed sticks. They have fasted to prepare for the game. Hunger makes them light and quick as deer. Some wear feathers in their hair from birds with *sharp eyesight and speed — important skills in Tewaarathon.*

The ball is tossed up. The team captains leap for it. The game is on! The old man smiles.

Tewaarathon was an important part of the culture of the Mohawk people. They believed the game was a gift from the Creator. They felt it had the power to heal sickness and conflict. In the Mohawk language, *Tewaarathon* means "little brother of war." If villages or nations argued, they would play Tewaarathon instead of fighting. The games could be rough, but not as rough as war. These matches were played by men, but women and children also played Tewaarathon for fun.

For hundreds of years before Europeans came to North America, First Nations people played different versions of the ball-and-stick game. In some regions, two sticks were used, with the ball held

A Tewaarathon game at the Mohawk village, near present-day Brantford, Ontario (mural by A. Jacobs)

between them. In others, the sticks had small, circular ends. Mohawk sticks looked like the wooden sticks that are still used today, with one end curved like a hook.

It took skill and patience to make a Tewaarathon stick. First, a long piece of hickory wood was softened with steam. Then, one end was bent into a hook and tightly tied. It had to stay like that for many months to hold its shape. Then the stick was carved, and leather strips were woven in the hook to make a webbed pocket.

Balls were made from animal skins stuffed with hair, moss, grass, or bark. In the Great Lakes region, balls were carved from knots of wood. Some had holes that whistled when they flew through the air to warn players that the ball was coming. Since they played with no helmets or pads, players did not want to get hit with a hard ball!

Most Tewaarathon players wore just a loincloth, with bare feet or moccasins. Body paint was used to mark teams. There was no such thing as "out of bounds" on the playing fields. If the ball went into the woods, the game would carry on there. Goals were up to a mile apart. Teams ranged from about 15 to hundreds of players, depending on the reason for the game. Before they began playing, teams would decide how many goals they had to score to win. Some games lasted all day, or even many days.

The games were huge social events. There was feasting and dancing. Friendships were made. Young people fell in love. Marriages were planned. Gambling was common. People bet furs, clothing, tools, and jewellery on their home teams to win. Gambling was a way of spreading skills. When people won well-made items, they learned how they were made.

The French missionaries who came to North America in the early 1600s called the game *la crosse*. People used to believe that they named the game after the shape of the stick. But now it is known that the name comes from "le jeu de la crosse," the French name for a game like field hockey. The missionaries did not approve of some aspects of the game. They wanted the Natives to believe that healing came from Christ, not lacrosse. They didn't like how

In the 1800s, lacrosse was played on ice in the winter.

rough the game was, and they thought gambling was a sin. But many early settlers liked the game very much. They played matches with each other, and with the Native people. In winter, they wore skates and played lacrosse on ice.

In 1849, a six-year-old boy from Montreal went to see a Mohawk lacrosse game with his dad. He loved the game and was soon playing lacrosse for hours with his friends at school. The boy's name was

George Beers. He would one day be called "the father of modern lacrosse."

As a teen, Beers felt the game could be improved. He thought the game should be more about brain-work and less about muscle. He wondered if the Natives always won because the playing field was long. The Natives could outrun the non-Natives and not get tired. Beers thought that if shorter playing fields were used, non-Native lacrosse players might have a better chance of winning. He made up other rules too, about the number of players, positions, and penalties. But Native teams still won the games. A Native team won when they played for the Prince of Wales during his 1860 visit to Montreal. In 1866, another team of Native players beat the Montreal Lacrosse Club to win the first Canadian championship.

When Canada became a country in 1867, Beers tried to get lacrosse named the national sport. Lacrosse was hugely popular. The number of lacrosse clubs had grown from just a few to 80. The National Lacrosse Association (NLA) was formed. Beers published a book called *Lacrosse: The National Game of Canada*. The book describes the history of the game and the new way of playing it. It also revealed Beer's racist feelings. "Civilized" non-Native lacrosse, he wrote, was a better game than "barbaric" Native lacrosse.

Canada's National Sport: Myth or Fact?

For more than 100 years, most Canadians believed lacrosse was Canada's national sport. But there was not actually any proof the government did make it official. In 1994, the government officially named lacrosse Canada's national summer sport. Hockey is the national winter sport.

Beers and others who loved lacrosse wanted to show it to the world. With the help of the NLA, they took teams of Native players and "Canadian gentlemen" on tour. The teams travelled through the United States and Britain. They played for Queen Victoria, and at the World's Fair in Paris. Crowds flocked to see real "sons of the forest," as Beers called the Natives. Europeans loved the exciting game. Soon they were playing lacrosse too.

In the world of lacrosse, players didn't always agree about money. Most Native players were professional or "pro" athletes, paid to play. Many could not afford to travel off the reserve to play non-Native teams unless they were paid. Non-Native amateur athletes had good jobs or were wealthy, so they didn't need the money. They thought their love of sport was purer, and did not like to compete with pro athletes.

In 1880, the NLA changed its name to the National *Amateur* Lacrosse Association (NALA). They banned Native pros from being members and competing for championships. Native teams continued playing with each other, and they played at the Olympics in 1904. (Two Canadian teams won medals: the Montreal Shamrocks won gold, and the Six Nations Mohawks won the bronze.) But most of the time, Native lacrosse teams could not compete in the sport their ancestors had invented.

In the early 1900s, lacrosse was so popular that there were trading cards of the best players. It was a favourite sport at many colleges. But over the years, the sport grew more violent. Fans were rowdy. Games often ended in fights and arrests. Some amateur lacrosse players were paid in secret. Some clubs hired light-skinned Native players as "ringers" to help their non-Native teams win. All these factors gave lacrosse a bad name.

In the 1930s, a Canadian invention gave lacrosse a much-needed boost. Box lacrosse, or "boxla" for short, was a form of lacrosse played in an enclosed "box." This indoor version of the game was developed as a way to use hockey arenas in the off-season. It was also played in outdoor "boxes."

Box lacrosse is a faster game because the ball bounces off the boards and is in almost constant play. There is more passing, checking, and teamwork in a smaller area, because players aren't running the length of a large field. In field lacrosse, the playing area is about the size of a football field (100 metres by 64 metres or 328 feet by 210 feet.) In box lacrosse, the floor is less than a quarter that size (60 metres by 25 metres or 197 feet by 82 feet.) Lower-level leagues play on even smaller floors in local hockey arenas. It takes great skill to score, since the goal net is much smaller than field lacrosse nets.

Fans loved to see box lacrosse players charge up and down the floor, flinging the ball back and forth and firing it into the small corners of the goal. It soon became Canada's most popular type of lacrosse. Other countries focused on field lacrosse, but Canadians became masters of the box.

2 First There Was Ross

One day, Gaylord Powless would rule the box. But someone came before Gaylord, and was his inspiration. That man was his father, Ross Powless.

Born on the Six Nations of the Grand River Territory in 1926, Ross grew up in a family of lacrosse players. As a boy, he watched his father, uncles, and grandfather play lacrosse on the reserve. The games were big social events. Brass bands played and crowds gathered to cheer their teams.

Ross later said, "People would walk in from miles around in them days to see lacrosse … Between periods us kids would pick up the lacrosse sticks and race out onto the field to play. The referee would have a heck of a time getting the playing area cleared. Didn't matter none … nobody ever wanted those games to end."

Ross's Uncle Cec was on a team of Six Nations players that went to Atlantic City in 1932 to play top box lacrosse teams from Montreal, Toronto, and Boston. The Six Nations goalie, "Punch" Garlow, did not wear a mask, pads, or throat guard. Ross remembered him looking like a leopard, with black and blue bruises for spots.

When Ross was eight, two sad events stripped him of family and of lacrosse. His mother died, and he was taken from his home. At this time, Native children were forced to live at residential schools away from their families. Teachers tried to make

The Six Nations team that went to Atlantic City in 1932

the children forget their traditions. They were not allowed to speak their Native languages or play lacrosse. The schools were tough in other ways too. Often the children went hungry. They were forced to do hard physical work. Many were abused.

Ross left school at 14. Finally he could play lacrosse again, but he got mad easily and played rough. His dad took him aside and said, "You're not out there to injure people, you're out there to play your best and enjoy the game." Ross said his dad "loved the game so much he couldn't stand to see me abuse it in that way. From that time on, I started to become a different kind of player."

Ross studied the goalies on other teams to find their weaknesses. He learned all he could from his teammates, and made a lot of assists. He became known for his staying power. When other players got tired in the third period, Ross was still going strong. His secret was to train by running. Ross

Ross Powless (left) and a teammate in an outdoor lacrosse box

loved to run long distances. His father and uncles did too. It gave them strong lungs and legs for lacrosse.

In 1945, when Ross was 19, he headed west. He played for a Native team in British Columbia: the North Shore Indians. Ross learned a lot that year, especially from his coach, Andy Paull. "He'd been recruiting players from Six

Running Like Longboat

The Six Nations of the Grand River Territory was also home to Tom Longboat, a famous marathon runner. Born in 1884, Tom grew up playing lacrosse and running for fun. When he was a teen, he began winning races. At 19, he won the Boston Marathon. Each year, Tom Longboat Awards are given to top Native amateur athletes in Canada. Ross Powless won this award twice, and so did his son Gaylord.

Nations since the '30s," said Ross. "And he was a respected man all across Canada."

When the season ended, Ross headed to Buffalo to look for work. There he met the girl who would become his wife. Wilma Bomberry came from a family of lacrosse players too. They fell in love, and the next year, Gaylord Ross Powless was born.

3 Growing Up with Lacrosse

Lacrosse was a huge part of Gaylord's life. His dad, uncles, grandparents, and cousins played the sport. He grew up on stories about great lacrosse games and the men who played them.

Gaylord was skilled with a lacrosse stick, even as a toddler. He followed his dad everywhere and played lacrosse every chance he got. When Gaylord was three, his dad earned a spot on the Huntsville team. The family left the reserve and

Lacrosse is for the Birds

In one First Nations legend about lacrosse, four-legged land animals wanted to play lacrosse with the birds. Mouse and Squirrel were turned away by the land animals because they were too small. The birds made wings for Mouse out of drum leather, and he became a Bat. They stretched Squirrel's skin so he became a Flying Squirrel. Quick, clever, and sharp-sighted, Bat and Flying Squirrel helped the bird team win. This legend shows that in lacrosse — as in life — all play a part.

camped near Huntsville so they could see Ross play.

"Gaylord and I used to put on a little show for the fans in between the periods," Ross said. "I'd stand with my back to the net and he'd put a little shift on me and go in for the goal. Beat me every time!"

By 1951, five-year-old Gaylord was the

oldest of five Powless children. He could catch, pass, run, and score like a streak of lightning on two sturdy little legs. He was ready to play organized lacrosse.

He even scored in his very first game — but not the way he wanted to! The ball was in front of his own net, and when somebody shouted "Shoot!" Gaylord scored on his own goalie.

Gaylord was proud to have one of Canada's top lacrosse players as his dad. Ross's team, the Peterborough Timbermen, won the Mann Cup (Canada's top prize for senior men's lacrosse) in 1951, 1952, 1953, and 1954. Ross was named Most Valuable Player of the playoff series in 1953.

With so many kids, it became hard for the family to travel with Ross. Instead, they stayed at home on the Six Nations reserve. They lived on a beautiful piece of land with more than 24 hectares (60 acres) for hunting and fishing. Gaylord loved being able to catch food for the family's supper.

He was a big help to his mom in other ways too. The house had no running water or power. Wood had to be chopped for the wood stove. Water had to be pumped from the well, hauled to the house, and heated for cooking, laundry, and bathing. Gaylord helped with the cooking too. He was good at making big batches of stew. The kitchen table expanded so everyone could fit around it, each child in his or her special place. Then the family would dig in and share stories of their day. There were lots of jokes, laughter, and, of course, stories about lacrosse.

The talking and laughing lasted into the night when the kids went to bed, girls in one room, boys in another. Sometimes Ross's lacrosse buddies and their wives would gather in the kitchen to play music and rehash the games. Gaylord and the other kids would lie on their bellies upstairs, faces pressed to the heating vent so they could hear what was being said.

The family kept growing. Twins Richard and Victor were born in the spring of 1955. It was Gaylord's job to feed baby Victor. When he was only five months old, Victor caught pneumonia and died. Gaylord, who was only eight at the time, was crushed.

More babies followed the twins. Over the years, Gaylord became big brother to 12 Powless children: Gail, Gary, Audrey, Greg, Harry, Darryl, Arlene, Richard, Karen, Tony, Jeffrey, and Jacqui. They scrapped and argued as all siblings do, but they protected each other too. They walked to and from the one-room school together. They played lacrosse together. They worked together to help earn money for the family.

Gaylord's sister Audrey remembers picking fruit to make money for school clothes. "Gaylord was always a joker," she said. "He'd fling berries at me, and then pretend he hadn't done it." Gaylord's aim was perfect. All those years playing lacrosse helped.

Gaylord had a special place in his mother's heart. Audrey said, "He was one of her favourites, probably because he was her first-born child and because he loved her so much. There was nothing our mother would not do to help Gaylord with sports or school. She would drive him to his games and practices and always made sure he had money. She went without a lot of things to help Dad make sure that we all did well growing up."

To support his growing family, Ross became a carpenter and foreman. One of his building projects at home was a backdrop where the boys could play lacrosse. The backdrop was 12 metres (40 feet) wide by 6 metres (20 feet) tall, made

*Gaylord (sitting to the right of his mother at centre)
and his family at Christmas, in the late 1960s*

from wood and chicken wire. It had a real
lacrosse goal, with a marked crease and
shooting line.

"We practised plays until we got them
down," Gaylord's brother Richard said.
"Dad would come out and show us things.
Gaylord taught us about offence, especially
power plays. His backhand was so accurate,
he could flip the ball into your stick

without even looking." Gary was the goaltender in the family. "He and Gaylord would practise for hours, with Gaylord trying to score on him," said Audrey. "I believe this is one reason why Gary was such an amazing goaltender, because he played against the best."

The Powless house was filled with lacrosse sticks. Each Powless boy had two (a game stick and a spare). The girls had sticks for playing catch-and-throw. In the evenings, Gaylord and the other kids worked on their sticks with Ross, making the pockets deeper and adjusting the strings.

For a boy who loved lacrosse, it was a perfect life. Having Ross Powless for a dad was like having a live-in coach. Having lots of brothers and sisters was like having a live-in team. With the help of his loving family, Gaylord became one of the best young players on the reserve.

4 In the Box

Like many teens, Gaylord had his good days and bad days. Most of the time he was happy. He was fit and good-looking. He was a good son, brother, student, and lacrosse player. He worked hard and played hard.

Gaylord was a prankster, always having fun and making people laugh. But when he was 13, Gaylord became the butt of a joke. Almost overnight, his skin broke out in a bad case of eczema. The kids at school started calling him "Scabs." He hated the name and the way his skin looked, but he tried not to show how it bothered him. That's what you do on the lacrosse floor. Be tough. Don't show you're hurting.

Gaylord's feelings boiled below the surface. Sometimes they burst out of him in the arena. Lacrosse is a contact sport. It's a rough game with lots of checking. Gaylord got hit a lot, and hard. What did he do? He hit back even harder.

"I was kind of a hot-head," Gaylord said later. "If I got hit, I'd hit right back and get tossed out of the game."

Gaylord spent so much time in the penalty box that his mother said she would stop coming to his games. His dad's threat was even worse. If Gaylord didn't stop getting penalties, his dad was going to make him quit.

"Mom and Dad didn't believe in playing stupid and getting penalties," said

Gaylord's sister Gail. "I remember Dad saying, 'Don't lose your temper out there. When you lose your temper, your mind is out of the game.'"

Ross spoke from experience. Gaylord knew his dad had been a rough player as a teen. But Ross had learned to calm his anger and channel his energy. Gaylord tried to do the same. It wasn't easy. Keeping his temper was something he had to work on all the time. But the choice was clear. Control your temper or quit.

A Natural Penalty Box

One First Nations legend tells the story of a young lacrosse player who was rude and violent. He was warned to stop but would not. As punishment, he was thrown into a tree. His head stuck out one side and his feet stuck out the other. He stayed trapped like that for the rest of the game.

And quitting was the last thing Gaylord Powless wanted to do.

Like father, like son. Gaylord decided to become a different kind of player. He would no longer be the tough guy. He'd be the smart guy, a playmaker. He studied the other players. He learned how to set up his teammates so they could score. He helped the team work better as a whole.

Gaylord also trained hard. He ran with his brothers on the dusty roads around their home. That was another thing he learned from his dad — that running long distances would give him strong legs and lungs for lacrosse.

In the winter, to stay in shape, Gaylord played hockey. His lacrosse skills helped him become a great hockey player at the Junior level. But lacrosse was his first love.

When Gaylord was 16, he got to play lacrosse with the Hagersville Warriors, a Six Nations Intermediate team that his dad coached. Gaylord kept up with — and ran circles around — the older players. In the stands, a man named Jim Bishop watched him with interest.

Bishop was a sports broadcaster and coach of the hottest Junior A lacrosse team in Canada: the Oshawa Green Gaels. When Bishop had come to Oshawa four years earlier, lacrosse was almost dead in that city. His passion for the sport and his expert coaching brought it back to life. Bishop led the Gaels to win the Minto Cup — making them the Canadian champions of Junior A lacrosse. Now screaming fans packed the Oshawa Civic Auditorium. They even started fights if they couldn't get in to see the games.

Bishop saw Gaylord's raw talent. He knew Gaylord would be a great player for the Green Gaels. But Gaylord lived on the Six Nations reserve, many kilometres west of Toronto. The Green Gaels played in

Oshawa, many kilometres east of Toronto. At that time, Junior players were supposed to play for the team nearest their home. Otherwise, the home team had to sign a release form to let the player go to another team. In Gaylord's case, Bishop needed ten release forms from teams between the reserve and Oshawa. When he wanted something, Jim Bishop could not be stopped. Ten release forms? No problem.

5 Oshawa's New Star

Jim Bishop offered young Gaylord a spot on the Green Gaels team. But Gaylord wasn't allowed to say "yes" right away. His parents were worried. Gaylord was only 16. He would have to live far from home in a boarding house, and complete high school on his own. He wasn't used to the intense training and practice that went along with being a Junior A player. He had never even seen a Junior A game.

Ross took him to see the Gaels play the

Long Branch Junior A team. It was exciting lacrosse, with tough, speedy, highly-skilled players. Seeing them in action didn't scare Gaylord.

"I can play in this league," he insisted. Two hours later, he was on his way to Oshawa.

Life in Oshawa was very different from life on the Six Nations reserve. Gaylord not only got to play lacrosse every day, he *had* to. Jim Bishop was strict. If a player was late or missed a practice without a good excuse, he'd be suspended. The team practised every night, and sometimes more than that. Once they practised twice in one day and then played an exhibition game that night.

Bishop was also strict about the nightly curfew. Players had to be in bed early so they could get their rest. He even made bed checks to make sure his players weren't sneaking out. Gaylord's parents

The Oshawa Green Gaels. Gaylord is in the middle row, second from the left.

were strict too, but not like Jim Bishop.

When he was older, Gaylord said, "It was good for me at that stage of my life. I was young and needed that sort of direction." Bishop demanded respect from his players. They were loyal and gave him 100 percent of their effort on the lacrosse floor. There were perks too. The Gaels players got to ride to games in a team bus, and wear team jackets and ties. "It was high-class stuff for Gaylord," Ross said.

Gaylord worked hard to master the type of lacrosse Bishop taught. The Gaels were light on their feet, and always on the move. Fans liked the smart playmaking and speed of the "running game," as Bishop called it. Many people said it was "the fastest game on two feet."

Gaylord's instincts were amazing. He could tell where the ball was going to go, run to that spot, and quickly pass it or score. Gaylord wasn't a hard shooter, but he was accurate. He had one great shot that could fool a goalie. He could make the ball look like it was headed straight, but it would suddenly change direction and drop in the net.

Gaylord's first game with the Gaels was against the Long Branch team he'd seen with his dad. Gaylord poured everything he had into that game. He shone like a star.

The Long Branch coach, Morley Kells, remembered that night well. "Jim Bishop brought him out of the reserve and no one had seen him before. I said right then, 'There's one who's going to be great.'"

In his second game, against the Guelph Mohawks, Gaylord played even better. He scored the winning goal. Newspapers started writing about the hot new player, the son of the great Ross Powless.

Soon the Gaels were in first place in the league. They had won the Minto Cup the year before, and wanted another. Gaylord would help them win it. But first they had to win the Eastern Canadian championship, then beat the best team from Western Canada.

By August, the Green Gaels boasted a 22-game winning streak. After each game, Gaylord's name was in the newspapers. He was praised, along with other high scorers like John Davis, the team captain.

Davis had lineups of people waiting for his autograph after each game. Gaylord had a growing number of fans too.

The playoff opener for the Eastern championship was against the Alderwood Terriers. Five hundred people had to be turned away from the packed arena. Fans who couldn't get seats listened to a play-by-play broadcast of the game. Gaylord was one of the top scorers that night.

The Gaels easily won the best-of-seven series. Then they beat the Brampton Armstrongs in a four-game sweep and defended their title as the Eastern champs.

A few days later, Gaylord and the Gaels were off to British Columbia. They were playing the Western champs, the New Westminster Salmonbellies. The Salmonbellies were a strong team, and the first game was a close 13 to 12 win for the Gaels. The *Toronto Star* praised Gaylord for getting the faceoffs during the game. They said Gaylord was the main reason the Gaels won.

The Green Gaels won games two and three of the playoff finals, but the Salmonbellies took the fourth. The Gaels bounced back to win the series. The Minto Cup was theirs again!

In his first season playing Junior A lacrosse, Gaylord helped his team become the Canadian champs. He was awarded the Jim McConaghy Memorial Cup as the Most Valuable Player of the series. He was also named winner of the Tom Longboat Award for Canada's top Native athlete of the year.

Back home on the Six Nations reserve, Gaylord's family, friends, former teachers, and coaches were filled with pride. The boy from the reserve had become a star. He was showing the world what a Mohawk could do.

6 The Marvellous Mohawk

In October 1964, Gaylord played lacrosse in the famous Maple Leaf Gardens for 7,000 cheering fans. It was a benefit game to raise money for Jim Smith, a Junior player with the Mimico Mounties.

Earlier in the season, Jim had been hurt while playing a league game. He was running at the enemy goal, and lost his balance trying not to step in the crease. At that moment, head down and facing forward, he was checked hard into the boards. The blow broke his neck and damaged his spinal cord. He would never walk again.

Jim watched the game at the Gardens from a stretcher tucked out of sight. Most people didn't know he was there, and that's how he wanted it. The Canadian champs, the Green Gaels, played an all-star team of top players in the Eastern Division. Many sports celebrities also took part in the program. Former hockey and lacrosse great Newsy Lalonde scored a goal right from the faceoff circle!

The Gaels ended up losing the game, but the fundraiser was a success. Ticket sales raised more than $15,000 to help Jim in the next phase of his life. Hopefully, his spirits were raised too. It was like the long-ago days when First Nations people played Tewaarathon to help sick people feel better.

With Maple Leaf Gardens behind them

and the Minto Cup in their pockets, the Green Gaels had another job to do: high school. On the lacrosse floor, Gaylord was a star. At school, things didn't go as well.

"I was in grade 11 at the time," said Gaylord, "[but] I failed a year because the Oshawa school was so much different than the one I had been attending."

One of the best things about school was becoming friends with Bobby Orr. The young Parry Sound hockey player was living in Oshawa to play for the Oshawa Generals, the feeder team for the Boston Bruins of the NHL. Gaylord and Bobby had a class together and found they had a lot in common. Both lived away from home, loved sports, had to juggle school and practices, and were learning to cope with their growing fame.

When the 1965 lacrosse season started, the Green Gaels were in good shape. In June, they set an Ontario Lacrosse

Association scoring record for a single game, beating the Guelph Mohawks 43 to 4. Gaylord racked up goals and assists, well on his way to setting records of his own.

The Gaels snared the 1965 Eastern Canada title. On a 31-game winning streak, they headed into the Minto Cup playoffs. Once again they were up against the New Westminster Salmonbellies. The first game of the series was in Oshawa.

Cheerleaders behind the Oshawa bench kept up a high-pitched "battle howl," the *Globe and Mail* reported. Fans chanted for Gaylord, and he poured on the gas. It was like he had a sixth sense, knowing where the ball would go. Again and again, he drove at the enemy goal, deking out the Salmonbellies to score. Gaylord never let up, even when a Salmonbelly stick broke his nose! But the Gaels still lost 9 to 6.

"Oshawa Green Gaels are the runningest,

shootingest, bounce-controllingest junior lacrosse team," wrote Frank Orr in the *Toronto Star*. "But last night, before 2,429 of the hometown diehards here, [the] Gaels didn't run, shoot, or control the bounces ... Of the Gael forwards, only Gaylord Powless was able to control the ball in the New Westminster zone."

It didn't help that Gaels goalie Merv Marshall wasn't feeling well. Marshall was a skilled goalie, but sometimes his nerves affected his game. Gaylord had been bothered by his nervous stomach too. Once he even threw up on the bench. So he learned to be careful about what he ate before games.

The Gaels had other reasons for their less-than-stellar performance. The Western players were bigger than the Gaels, and most were older too. Only four Salmonbellies were under 18, and only four Gaels were over 18. Bishop said that was no excuse: "We simply need more players going full out."

But Bishop did object to the extra players the Salmonbellies added to their team for the playoffs. The extras were three top players from other teams in the Western league. Bishop insisted that the Gaels be allowed to borrow a player too. Billy Armour was a former Gael who had started playing for the team from Hastings, Ontario. He was an Ontario league scoring champion. With Armour back on the team, the Gaels prepared for game two.

Goalie Merv Marshall "faced enough rubber in practice to put new tires on half the cars in town," wrote Frank Orr. "And in Oshawa [car capital of Canada] that's saying something." Bishop had seven players shoot "at least a thousand times," at Merv. "It worked," Bishop said. "Merv got the touch back."

All the Gaels bounced back for the next game. The *Toronto Star* said it was "some of the finest lacrosse seen in the east in many years, with fancy passing and hard-checking by both clubs." Gaylord won the faceoffs, made four assists, and scored two goals – all this with a broken nose!

The Gaels poured it on hard for the rest of the series. Tight ball control and faceoff wins kept them in the lead. Gaylord's name appeared in glowing newspaper reports.

Trick Shot

Gaylord invented a move his brother Richard calls the "backhand bounce." As Gaylord drove in on the enemy goal, he would be swarmed by the other team. Quick as a blink, he would turn around. With his back to the net, he'd bounce the ball between his legs, right past the goalie — and score!

This line from the *Globe and Mail* sums him up: "When he was on the floor, the Salmonbellies were in trouble."

Gaylord helped the Gaels win the Minto Cup for the third year in a row, and he won the Ken Ross Trophy for his own skill and sportsmanship. It was a sweet reward for the boy who used to be a "hot-head."

Gaylord receiving the Advertiser Trophy for Top Scorer in the Junior A Series, 1966

7 Sticks and Stones

When Gaylord was a teen living at home, he liked to go out with friends and have fun. In Oshawa, under the watchful eye of Jim Bishop, he had less freedom. The nightly practices and early curfews got on his nerves.

As a sports star, Gaylord was popular with the guys. As a handsome young athlete, he was popular with the girls. He became known as a guy who liked to party. Several times, Bishop suspended

Gaylord from games because he missed practice or curfew. After a game in Montreal, Gaylord stayed out all night. As he was coming in, all dressed up from the night before, he ran into his coach.

"You're off the club for breaking curfew," Bishop said.

Gaylord responded as quickly as he would on the lacrosse floor. "You don't know if I'm coming or going," he said.

Talking back to his coach showed a lot of nerve. Gaylord's brother Richard says, "Dad would tell us, 'It doesn't matter if you think you know more than the coach, or even if you *do* know more than the coach, you never talk back.' If Dad saw you mouthing off to the coach, he'd yank you out and say 'You're not going to the next five games!'"

Gaylord was a valuable member of the team, but Bishop believed rules were for everyone. If Gaylord wanted to play lacrosse, he had to live by the rules. If not, he'd be thrown off the team. Finally, Bishop agreed to let Gaylord stay with the club if he paid a fine of $200 for staying out all night. The money would be held in trust until the end of the season. If Gaylord did anything else wrong, he'd lose the money — and his place on the team.

"He wanted to play so bad, that's how we disciplined him," said Bishop. "He had to do things our way."

Gaylord faced conflict on the lacrosse floor too. Racist players called him names, insulting his Native heritage. In one town, people threw drinks at him through the chicken wire above the boards. Gaylord tried to ignore the taunts. People wouldn't act like that, he thought, if he wasn't beating them. "If you carry the ball," he said, "you're a natural target."

Gaylord's teammates called him names too: "Indian," "Iroquois," "Comanche," and "Chief." Often they told him to "scalp" or "tomahawk" an opponent. Today, those comments would not be allowed. But at the time, Gaylord said, "There are two types of kidding. One kind is all in fun and I give it right back … I get some from the other teams [too]. That's different. It's more than needling but it doesn't bother me. … All we ask [as Natives] is that we be judged … as individuals, not just called 'Indian' in a distasteful way."

Sometimes it was the reporters who made racist comments. They called him "full-blooded Indian" and described him as having "fast moccasins." One reporter made fun of Gaylord's name as being oddly "elegant" for a Native. (Gaylord's mother, Wilma, was an avid reader. When she found the name in a book, she liked it enough to give it to her first-born child.)

The old saying goes: "Sticks and stones

Proud to Be a Mohawk

The press and fans called Gaylord the "Marvellous Mohawk." Did it bother him that the nickname referred to his Native background? "I don't think he minded," says his brother Richard. "He was very proud of his heritage."

may break my bones ... but names will never hurt me." Gaylord found himself the target of sticks — pounding, slashing lacrosse sticks — during every game. Gaylord was a high scorer and made many assists. Other teams knew they had a better chance of winning if they got Gaylord out of the game. With his amazing reflexes, Gaylord got away from most of his attackers. When they did make contact, he didn't let on how badly they hurt him. Gaylord wore braces with steel plates to help soften the blows when they slashed his knees.

"He had an inner toughness … " said Bishop. "He was able to take a lot of punishment … he actually reacts better when he's being knocked around."

In the 1966 Minto Cup playoffs, the Green Gaels again clashed sticks with the New Westminster Salmonbellies. The western team had lots of tough, fight-loving players. The *Toronto Star* reported: "One of the big reasons for New Westminster's penalties was Gaylord Powless, Oshawa's big, burly full-blooded Indian centre, who had several over-eager New Westminster players sent to the penalty box when they checked him too hard."

This was Gaylord's strategy: don't fight back when other players slash and check. That way, his opponent would get the penalty and the Gaels could score on the power play.

In another game, two Salmonbellies were told to rough up Gaylord. Paul and

John Shmyr were brothers who went on to play in the National Hockey League. They called Gaylord names to get him to react, but he ignored them. Paul Shmyr hit him on the lip with his stick and cut it badly. Instead of fighting back, Gaylord spit blood on Shmyr's face. In a rage, Schmyr slashed Gaylord and was given a penalty. With the Salmonbellies short-handed, the Gaels popped in a couple of goals and won the game.

Gaylord wondered later if he should have been thrown out of the game for spitting blood. He admitted he wasn't perfect. Sometimes he did lose his temper. Most times, though, he got back at abusive players by checking them legally and scoring on their net. Gaylord had learned this lesson years before: the best revenge is to play well and win the game.

Gaylord and the Gaels won the Minto Cup again. It was the fourth Cup in a row for the Gaels, and the third one for Gaylord. Three years playing Junior. Three national championships. But there was more. For the second time, Gaylord won the Ken Ross Trophy for skill and sportsmanship. He also won the Advertiser Trophy as Top Scorer in a Junior A Series for his 17 goals and 31 assists. During the season, Gaylord had scored 71 goals and made 120 assists. His total points earned for the 1966 Junior A season was a whopping 191 — a new Canadian record.

8 Canada's Team Player

Gaylord had become a superstar in Oshawa. Fans came by the thousands to see him play. He was often compared to Oshawa's other young superstar, Bobby Orr. Bobby had just left for Boston to play for the Bruins.

Close ties to his family kept Gaylord's feet on the ground. His brothers started playing Junior lacrosse as well. Greg and Harry played for Port Credit, and Gary played for Long Branch. Ross said he and

Gaylord practising with the Green Gaels for a spot on Team Canada, 1967

Wilma "racked up a lot of miles" travelling to their sons' games. With help from Gail and Wilma, Ross collected statistics on the opponents' teams. For every game, Ross knew who scored and made assists, who won faceoffs, and who got penalties. This helped his sons know which players to watch and which to avoid.

In the spring of 1967, Gaylord played at two important meets: Expo 67, and the International Lacrosse Tournament. Expo 67 was a huge World's Fair held in Montreal. Visitors could try food, music, arts, games, and sports from all over the globe. Those who couldn't attend watched on TV. About 700 million people watched or listened to the opening ceremonies via satellite.

Lacrosse Around the World

By the 1970s, lacrosse was being played around the world. The International Lacrosse Federation was formed in 1974. Full-member nations now include Australia, Canada, the Czech Republic, England, Germany, Ireland, Iroquois Nationals, Japan, Korea, New Zealand, Scotland, Sweden, United States, and Wales.

At Expo, the North American All-Indian Lacrosse Tournament let visitors see the game invented by First Nations people. Canada's team was coached by Ross Powless. Gaylord was a player, along with men from the Six Nations and Akwesasne reserves.

The tournament was field lacrosse, since that sport was more like the traditional Native game. Gaylord was not used to the rules, playing area, and player positions of field lacrosse. But he practised and learned and, as always, played well. Canada beat the United States in all three games, but really it was a win for First Nations people in both countries. For hundreds of years, Native athletes had played lacrosse to strengthen friendships with other nations. At Expo, modern Native players achieved the same thing on a grand scale. They made friends with the world.

Right after Expo, Gaylord played at the International Lacrosse Tournament. Canada was 100 years old in 1967. The lacrosse match was one of the Centennial events. They played field lacrosse. Box lacrosse hadn't taken off in other countries the way it had in Canada.

Top lacrosse players arrived from the United States, England, and Australia. The teams from England and Australia were all-star squads. The United States sent their national champs: Mount Washington of Baltimore. Canada's team was made up of box lacrosse players from the Peterborough Petes (the Senior Canadian champs), plus four Green Gaels Junior stars. One of them was Gaylord. Canada's team coach was Bobby Allen of Peterborough, and Jim Bishop of the Green Gaels was assistant coach.

The four nations met to decide on the rules. "Some of the strange rules, which

Canadians haven't worried about since 1934, concern the width of nets, the width and length of sticks, off-sides and poke-checking," wrote the *Globe and Mail.* "However, players won't have to keep both hands on the stick as they do in Australia, England, and the United States."

The round-robin tournament took place in Toronto and three Ontario hotbeds of lacrosse: Peterborough, Fergus, and St. Catharines. Canada won their first game in Peterborough against England, 11 to 8. Gaylord scored the first goal after just 44 seconds. In spite of rain, a crowd of 3,000 watched the rough game. 54 penalties were called, 31 against Canada.

The next two games didn't go well. Canada lost to Australia 18 to 10 in another rough game. Even Gaylord lost his temper. He got a penalty for taking a poke at an Australian who had slashed him. Then Canada came up against the highly favoured United States team. Canada started out strong, leading 5 to 3 after the first period. Gaylord played well and scored twice, but in the end Canada lost 18 to 7.

The United States won the gold medal, Australia placed second, and Canada took the bronze. It was embarrassing for the Canadians, but they had an excuse. Box lacrosse was their game, not field lacrosse. At least they hadn't come in last!

Through all this, Gaylord still played for

Field Champs Again!

The International Lacrosse Tournament got Canadians interested in field lacrosse again. By 2007, Canada was the world champ in both indoor (box) and field lacrosse. Gaylord's son, Chris, was a superb defenceman in field lacrosse. He played for Canada at two world championships.

the Green Gaels. It was his last season of Junior lacrosse and he wanted it to be great. Another Minto Cup win would do the trick. Once again, it was the New Westminster Salmonbellies who challenged the Gaels for the Cup. Fans and sports writers called Gaylord "the man to watch."

"If [the] New Westminster Salmonbellies hope to stop the Oshawa Green Gaels …," wrote the *Toronto Star,* "they're going to have to find a formula to stop Gaylord Powless." Their formula, as the *Star* put it, was "Stop Powless, stop Gaels." Some said it seemed more like "Kill Powless." Gaylord had two or three Salmonbellies on him all the time. It's a wonder he ever got the ball. But he did get the ball — and a whole lot of injuries.

Gaylord was playing with a taped back, a hurt calf, and a throbbing finger. "Nobody would know he was 5-feet-11 of pain," wrote the *Star.* In every game, he scored goals and made assists, "which is pretty good from inside a bundle of tape."

As always, Gaylord kept his cool. In one game, he swooped past the enemy goal on a scoring attempt. A Salmonbelly named Al Lethwaite ran at him full speed and crashed him into the boards. Gaylord almost passed out. Moments later, he limped to the bench with his calf in bad shape. But in the final period, he was playing again. Three times, the *Star* wrote, he could have "flattened Lethwaite. He played the ball instead."

Gaylord led the Gaels to another Minto Cup win. It had been four incredible years. With the Gaels, Gaylord won four Minto Cups. He was two-time winner of several awards: the Advertiser Trophy for Top Scorer, the Jim McConaghy Memorial Cup for Most Valuable Player, the Ken Ross Trophy for skill and sportsmanship, and the Tom Longboat Award for being

Canada's Native athlete of the year. He set scoring and assist records. He was chosen for several all-star teams, and played for Team Canada at two major series.

By the end of his Junior career, Gaylord wasn't sure what to do. If his game was hockey instead of lacrosse, he could get a $50,000 deal to turn pro. Pro lacrosse didn't offer that kind of money. It hardly offered any money at all. That didn't matter to Gaylord. He loved the game and would play no matter what. But he needed a job to support himself. He decided to follow in his father's footsteps once again, and became a carpenter.

9 Turning Pro

In 1968 Gaylord was invited to play pro lacrosse for an American team called the Detroit Olympics. It was a season of firsts — new league, new team, new level of play, new rules. But some of the faces were the same. The new National Lacrosse Association (NLA) was the idea of Green Gaels coach Jim Bishop and Morley Kells, who had coached the Long Branch Junior team and saw Gaylord play his first game as a Junior.

Bishop was manager-coach of the Detroit team. Many of his players, like Gaylord, were "grads" from the Oshawa Gaels. Some Junior players were allowed to play up to 12 games for the pro teams. The Olympics practised in Oshawa and drove to Detroit for games.

Many people thought the new pro league would flop. But the NLA planned to succeed. They were careful not to spend too much money. Luckily, the players settled for low pay. They loved the game and being able to play at a high level was reward enough. The clubs helped players get jobs that would let them get to practices and games.

To make lacrosse more exciting to watch, the NLA set new rules. The "45-second rule" meant a team had to try to score within 45 seconds of getting the ball. If it didn't, the ball went to the other team. There would be no more defence players unless a team was short-handed on a power play and needed to guard their net. "At all other times," said Kells, "it must be man on man. We don't want people standing around. We want to emphasize speed." Bishop set up TV and radio spots to promote the "new lacrosse."

The new league had eight teams in two divisions. The Eastern Division was made up of the Detroit Olympics, Toronto Maple Leafs, Peterborough Lakers, and Montreal Canadiens. Western teams were the Vancouver Canucks, Victoria Shamrocks, New Westminster Salmonbellies, and Portland Adanacs. Eastern and Western teams would play all through the season, not just at playoff time.

At the season opener, Gaylord got another chance to play at the famous Maple Leaf Gardens. Bishop's Detroit Olympics beat Kells's team, the Toronto Maple Leafs. Gaylord scored only one goal, but he won

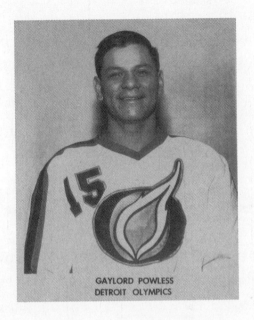

GAYLORD POWLESS
DETROIT OLYMPICS

Gaylord Powless made the number 15 famous.

the faceoffs and set up lots of great plays. "We can't let Gaylord (Powless) control the ball as much as he did," Kells told the *Toronto Star*. But they couldn't stop him. Gaylord's ability to win faceoffs, control the ball, and set up plays led the Detroit Olympics to first place in the Eastern Division.

At the end of July, the team ran into trouble. A brutal check left Gaylord with a badly hurt shoulder. The doctors said he'd be out of action for three to four weeks. Then the Olympics lost one of their Junior whiz kids, Ross Jones, because he had played his quota of 12 games.

Gaylord was never one for lying around. Two weeks after being hurt he was up and running. He scored four goals in his first game back. The public loved Gaylord. And they loved the new style of lacrosse — until football season started. Just when the lacrosse playoffs began, sports fans were glued to their TVs watching football. The NLA knew TV was key to the success of pro lacrosse. They did get some games televised, but not enough. The numbers of fans at playoff games dropped. The only team that didn't lose money during the season was New Westminster.

The Detroit Olympics beat the Peterborough Lakers to win the Eastern Division title. It was an exciting series — for those who saw it. New Westminster won the Western Division finals. After four years of facing — and beating — the Junior Salmonbellies for the Minto Cup,

Mr. Hockey or Mr. Lacrosse?

While he was in Detroit, Gaylord got to know Gordie Howe, who played for the Detroit Red Wings in the NHL. When the ice was in the arena, Gaylord skated with Gordie. When the ice was out, Gaylord taught him how to play lacrosse. The player known as Mr. Hockey was a natural. "The first week Gordie started off a right-hand player," Ross said. "By the second week he was switching hands as if he'd been doing it for years. After a month he could throw the ball from one end of the floor to the other and hit the net with either hand."

Gaylord faced his old rivals again. The Olympics won the first game 21 to 12. It looked like it was going to be a rerun of past years. But the Salmonbellies bounced back and won the best-of-seven series four games to two.

It was a year of highs and lows. On a blind date, Gaylord fell for a lovely girl named Laurie Bak. Soon they were married and expecting a baby. Their daughter Michelle was born in January 1969. Another highlight was when Gaylord was named Oshawa's Athlete of the Year. The *Oshawa Times* called Gaylord "the greatest athlete to perform in Oshawa in recent years, including Bobby Orr"!

A low point for Gaylord was finding that the public kept changing its mind about lacrosse. Sometimes thousands of fans packed the arenas. Sometimes there were only a couple of hundred — not enough to keep the league afloat. After only one year, the National Lacrosse Association went belly up.

The next year, Bishop and Kells worked to get the NLA running again. Meanwhile, Gaylord and Ross got offers from the Rochester team of the New York pro

Not Enough Sticks

Pro lacrosse had to fight for fans, but kids loved playing the sport. In 1968, more than 45,000 boys were registered in Ontario minor lacrosse. Native stick-makers had trouble keeping up with the demand. Companies began making plastic and fibreglass sticks that Gaylord and his dad called "Tupperware," named after the plastic boxes used for storing food. Gaylord always played with a wooden stick. In later years, Ross would send Native-made sticks to any of Gaylord's teammates who wanted them.

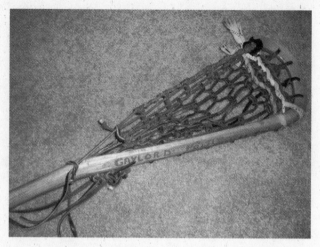

One of Gaylord's lacrosse sticks. He always used a traditional wooden stick.

lacrosse league. Soon they were off to New York: Gaylord as player, Ross as coach. Ross brought Gaylord's brothers Greg and Harry to play for Rochester too. Harry was tall with long strides and a long reach. He was a "finesse player" like Gaylord, good at fancy stickwork and tricky plays. Greg was a tough defensive player, and hard to beat.

The Rochester players respected Ross and worked hard for him. One player said he learned more in one year from Ross than in all the years he played before that. Ross didn't give out a lot of praise. His sons were used to that. If a player did well, Ross might muss his hair when he came back to the bench. But the only time he'd say much was when the player did something wrong. Gaylord was quiet too. But, as a former teammate said, "When Gaylord spoke, you listened."

10 *At Home and Away*

In the 1970s, Gaylord moved around a lot. As the *Globe and Mail* put it, he rarely spent "more than a season in one city, as lacrosse teams — and entire leagues — folded beneath him."

From 1970 to 1972, Gaylord played for the Brantford Warriors, a Senior lacrosse team Ross helped get started. Morley Kells was the coach. Kells tried to get sponsors so the team could play in Toronto. He believed that for lacrosse to be a mainstream sport, it needed the support of major cities. But the yo-yo of public support was at a low point. No matter. Wherever they were, Gaylord and the other players at the Senior/pro level treated their fans to superb lacrosse.

The Warriors did well in 1970, but just missed getting into the Mann Cup finals. It was Peterborough that faced Gaylord's old rivals, the New Westminster Salmonbellies.

Gaylord, centre, playing for the Brantford Warriors

But Gaylord himself won a victory. He received the Bucko McDonald Trophy as Top Scorer in the Ontario Lacrosse Association, with 142 points in just 23 games.

In the winter, Gaylord played hockey for the Six Nations Mohawks in the All-Ontario Indian Tournament. The Mohawks won the championship, and Gaylord was named Most Valuable Player. Gaylord had never given up his hockey. He played at Junior, Intermediate, and Senior levels, and won a few provincial titles. If he had wanted to, Gaylord probably could have become a pro hockey player.

"I guess I liked lacrosse better," he told the *Globe and Mail*, "probably because I was better at it than hockey." He didn't resent the fame and high salaries hockey players could earn. "Anybody who can attract crowds and bring in X number of dollars to the entertainment industry deserves everything he can get. I just wish it had happened to me in lacrosse."

In 1971, the Warriors played so well as a team, they were almost unbeatable. They were great friends as well as teammates. Warrior Bruce Todman said he was at the Powless house so much, he almost lived there. "I went to war with him [Gaylord] for 10 years," he told *The Expositor*.

Skills for All Seasons

Many lacrosse players play hockey, and many hockey players play lacrosse. The skills they learn and use in one game help them play the other. As a boy, Wayne Gretzky played lacrosse every summer in his hometown of Brantford, near the Six Nations reserve. Other hockey/lacrosse players include Don Cherry, Paul Coffey, Doug Gilmour, Tim Hunter, Paul Kariya, Joe Nieuwendyk, Adam Oates, Colin Patterson, and Gary Roberts.

"Unfortunately, four were against him but six were with him and those six were the best of my life as far as lacrosse goes. … [Gaylord] was a fierce competitor but … he taught me a lot about family and loyalty."

Gaylord was a high scorer, but he wasn't a ball hog. He constantly set up plays that made his teammates look good. Fellow Warrior Rick Dudley said, "If you made yourself open, you were going to get the ball."

Gaylord was the first on his team to perfect the new "quarterback" position. As in football, the lacrosse quarterback would set the pace and direction of the attack. "No one else could play it the way [Gaylord] did," Coach Kells told *The Expositor*. "I used to say he could play in a phone booth. He could take a pass and move it to the right guy in less than a step."

An example of Gaylord's skill came in a 1971 Mann Cup playoff game against the New Westminster Salmonbellies. "Somebody took a shot that missed the net and the ball came off the backboard like a bullet," Kells said. "Gaylord, about where the hockey blue line would be, took the rebound and fired it back into the net before the goalie could turn around. Only a player with Gaylord's skills could do that."

Those amazing plays added up to a Mann Cup victory for the Warriors in 1971. Gaylord matched the record he had set the year before — 17 points in a single game. Now he was a Senior Canadian champ as well as a former Junior Canadian champ. Best of all, he was able to play lacrosse while being close to his family.

On the reserve, the old house where Gaylord grew up was torn down. His parents' new house had all the modern comforts. Some things, though, stayed the same. The big kitchen table was put in the new house. When the family gathered for holidays, they sat in their same old spots. It was like old times. Lots of fun, food, laughter, love, and, of course, stories about lacrosse.

For the next few years, Gaylord moved from city to city to play lacrosse. "Had to go where the bucks were," he told the *Globe and Mail*. He played in Coquitlam, Syracuse, Montreal, Brampton ... Wherever he went, crowds came to see the Marvellous Mohawk in action. People said it was "magic" how he seemed to know what was going on everywhere at once. They said he handled the stick so well, it looked like it was part of his arm.

Being on the road was hard on Gaylord's marriage. He and Laurie divorced in 1973. Michelle still adored her handsome, famous dad and went to every game she could. At one thrilling game in Montreal, she got to be on TV with her dad and his old friend Bobby Orr.

In 1973, Gaylord called his brother Richard from British Columbia. Tryouts for a local Junior team were starting. Did Richard want to come and try out? Richard jumped at the chance. Just like when Gaylord went to Oshawa as a teen, waivers had to be signed. This time there were a lot more than ten teams between the Six Nations reserve and Coquitlam, British Columbia. No problem. Ross was a Hall of Famer. Everyone knew and respected him. He got the waivers signed and Richard was on his way. Richard made the team easily, wowing the coach with plays he'd learned from Gaylord and Ross.

In 1974, Gaylord got to play with five of his brothers on a team coached by their dad. "Maybe my boys never knew it," Ross said later, "but one of my biggest thrills was coaching six of them on one team at the North American Indian Lacrosse Tournament." Teams of First Nations players came from all over Canada and the United States to British Columbia to play. The Ontario team included the six older Powless boys: Gaylord, Gary, Greg, Harry, Richard, and Darryl. (Darryl was the youngest at 17. Tony and Jeffrey were too young to play.)

The Powless boys had a ton of fun playing together. "It was like being in the backyard again," said Richard. They knew each other's moves. They used plays they had practised for years. Each shift they scored goals. "It was perfect lacrosse, great teamwork," said Richard. "No prima donnas running down the floor, just everyone working together."

Harry liked it so much in western Canada that he stayed to play lacrosse for the North Shore Indians. Richard also

Gaylord and five of his brothers played on the Six Nations team coached by their father. From left to right: Harry, Gary, Darryl, Ross, Gaylord, Greg, Richard.

played in British Columbia for a while, for the North Shore Indians and New Westminster. Gaylord, though, was on the move again.

In 1975, he played for Montreal, then returned home to play for Six Nations in 1976, and Brampton in 1977. That was

Gaylord's last season. He was only 30 years old, but 14 years of slashing and pounding on cement floors was enough. His knees and back couldn't take any more abuse.

Gaylord retired with exactly 1,000 career goals and assists.

11 Giving Back to the Game

Ross Powless always said, "You have to give back to the game." For more than 20 years, Gaylord coached various levels of youth lacrosse in Brantford, Milton, and Six Nations. He was a natural coach. He taught his players skills and plays not often seen at their level of lacrosse. Like his old coach, Jim Bishop, Gaylord inspired his players to give their best effort.

"Boys, you can be stars," he told them. "This is your chance to shine."

And they did. The teams Gaylord coached always did well. Many won championships.

Gaylord married again in 1979. He and his new wife Patti lived on the Six Nations reserve. Their son Chris was born in 1981, and their daughter Gaylene followed in 1984. Both kids were playing with lacrosse sticks as soon as they could hold them. Gaylord worked as a carpenter. In his spare time, he coached lacrosse, hunted, fished, and spent time with family. His brother Gary and his family lived right next door.

Then Gaylord hurt his already damaged back. Surgery made it worse, and Gaylord had to retire from his job. Patti worked as a nurse, while Gaylord raised the kids at home. Gaylene says he was a great dad, "a big softie," and lots of fun. He loved to play pranks on the kids and joke with their friends.

As Chris's lacrosse coach, he was more serious. Like Ross, Gaylord didn't give his son a lot of direct praise. But Gaylene often heard him praising Chris to Patti. "You should have seen him play today!" he'd say.

Gaylord never truly hung up his lacrosse stick. He played Oldtimer lacrosse for fun and exercise. With his bad back and knees, he couldn't run. But he could still do amazing things with his stick. His friends teased him about being a "cherry-picker," a player who stays near the enemy goal, waiting for a pass so he can score.

During these years, the honours for Gaylord's lacrosse feats rolled in. In 1990, he joined his father as a member of the Canadian Lacrosse Hall of Fame. In 1992, Canada's Governor General presented him with a medal. When the Ontario Lacrosse Hall of Fame opened in 1996, Gaylord was made a member, along with Ross. They were the first father and son to be members of both Halls of Fame. And in 1997, the Canadian Lacrosse Association renamed the Junior A award for the most sportsmanlike player. It is now the Gaylord Powless Trophy.

Gaylord made a lasting impact on lacrosse in many ways. For decades, players have tried to copy his famous moves. There was the "hop," to fool players about which way he was going to go. And his "curve ball" that flew straight, then dropped in the net. And of course, his "backhand bounce," the backward shot that bounced between his legs and into the goal.

Gaylord showed that lacrosse players didn't have to be the biggest, toughest, or fastest to be the best. He showed kids that using your brain and controlling your emotions was important too.

He worked with a committee to make sure other Native lacrosse players got into the Halls of Fame. He tried to make lacrosse a mainstream pro sport — and now it is. But the most important way Gaylord gave back to the game may be how he bridged the two cultures that played lacrosse: the Native athletes who invented the game, and the non-Native players who adopted it. One of the original goals of lacrosse was to heal nations and strengthen friendships. Canada's people — Native and non-Native — needed that, and Gaylord helped make it happen.

12 The Final Battle

All his life, Gaylord fought battles. As a boy, he fought to conquer his temper and feelings of low self-esteem. As a teen, he fought to juggle school, sports, and fun with the rules. As a man, he fought for the sport he loved to play. As a Native lacrosse player, he battled players who attacked him because of his race and skill. And as a coach, he led hundreds of young lacrosse warriors into battle on the floor.

From 1999 to 2001, Gaylord battled an enemy more powerful than any he had faced before: cancer. Gaylord did not want to die. He fought back with surgery, medical treatments, and Native medicine. Gaylord was told he would live only a few months to a year, but he kept up the fight for much longer.

During Gaylord's first year with cancer, his daughter Michelle gave birth to a baby girl named Taylor. Gaylord adored his "Taylord," as he called her.

"That summer we followed my dad and brother to every game we could," Michelle said. Gaylord and his friend Jim Leeworthy were coaching Chris's Junior B team, the Milton Mavericks. They just missed getting into the Founders Cup final. Chris was upset; he had tried so hard to win for his dad. But Gaylord was hugely proud of his son. He said he'd never seen Chris play as well as he did that season.

As Gaylord's illness grew worse, he had to spend more time in bed. His lacrosse stick was propped nearby where it would give him strength. The closeness of family and friends gave him strength too.

"When we arrived for a visit," Michelle said, "Dad would yell 'Where's my baby!' Taylor would go barrelling into [Dad's] room and jump on his bed to snuggle."

Gaylene, a grade-nine student, gave up figure skating and missed a lot of school so she could be with her dad. Chris came home from college. Patti took care of Gaylord at home. The family would gather around Gaylord's bed with photo albums, laughing and joking about happy memories.

Sometimes lacrosse friends would visit. Gaylord loved talking about games played long ago. Ross joked that the memories of "us old lacrosse warriors" were hazy. "The older we get," he laughed, "the better we was."

Gaylord's grandson David (Michelle's son) was born in February 2001. From his bed, Gaylord signed David's first lacrosse stick.

Just days before his death, Gaylord found out that the Six Nations Arena, where he had played and coached for so

Some of Gaylord's sisters and their families at the Gaylord Powless Arena

many years, would be renamed the Gaylord Powless Arena. He was too sick to talk, but gave a big thumbs-up.

On July 28, 2001, Gaylord lost the battle with cancer. He was buried with lacrosse sticks, and wore a traditional Ribbon shirt with lacrosse sticks stitched on it. Tucked

The Best of the Past and Present

Lacrosse is still played in the Gaylord Powless Arena. Six Nations players also practise in the Iroquois Lacrosse Arena (ILA), a state-of-the-art, pro-size lacrosse arena. Teams from across the country, including the Toronto Rock, practise at the ILA, which is also home to the Powless Lacrosse Store. The store stocks the latest lacrosse gear, but remembers its roots. Near the shiny black and pink titanium sticks hang traditional wooden sticks made with patience and skill by Six Nations craftsmen.

in his hand was a lacrosse ball signed by his Oldtimers team. After his death, the newspapers and Internet were filled with stories about the Marvellous Mohawk. Coaches, teammates, players, fans, and sportswriters shared their memories of his great lacrosse career.

Ross died just two years later in 2003. He, too, was buried with lacrosse sticks. In an interview with CBC not long before his death, Ross said he was looking forward to playing lacrosse again with his family members who had passed on.

Gaylord's family continues to grow. Many are following in his footsteps onto the lacrosse floor. His son, grandsons, nephews, and great-nephews are superb lacrosse players. Gaylord's young cousin Delby Powless Jr. now plays pro lacrosse for the Buffalo Bandits. (Gaylord and Delby's father had coached him at the Midget level.) Other boys are playing

David Ross Anderson wears his grandfather Gaylord's number 15 to play lacrosse.

Tyke, Midget, Junior, and Intermediate lacrosse. Some have proudly worn Gaylord's famous number 15.

One number 15 is Gaylord's grandson, David. Like Gaylord, David has been a skillful lacrosse player from an early age. He has vivid dreams of playing lacrosse with his "Papa" Gaylord. Sometimes David will make an amazing play during a game, and his family asks, "Where did you learn that?" David's reply is, "Papa taught me."

"David was only a baby when my dad died," said Michelle. "I was so sad that he'd never be able to teach my son how to play lacrosse. I was wrong."

Gaylord also appears in the dreams of his daughter Gaylene's son, Kahner (born in 2004), and his sister Gail's grandson, Phoenix (born in 2003).

Whether or not you believe in spirits, when you watch these boys play, it's easy to see how Gaylord inspires them. In the Powless family, on the Six Nations reserve and in arenas across the country, Gaylord's legacy lives on.

Glossary

All-star teams: teams made of the best players from different teams

Amateur: an athlete who is not paid for playing a sport

Assist: a pass that sets up a goal

Bounce shot: a shot on goal that bounces before the goal line

Box: the enclosed area where *box lacrosse* is played

Boxla: short form for *box lacrosse*

Box lacrosse: indoor lacrosse played in arenas or in outdoor boxes

Centre: the *box lacrosse* offensive player who faces off

Check: to try to dislodge the ball from another player's stick by poking or bumping their stick or arms

Cherry-picker: a player who stays in the offensive end waiting for a long pass so he or she can score

Cradle: to carry the ball while running, using a side-to-side motion to keep it in the webbing of the lacrosse stick

Crease: the area in front of a goal

Cross-check: with both hands on the shaft of the stick, hitting another player with the area of the stick between the hands

Defence: the players who try to keep the other team from scoring

Draw: another word for *faceoff*

Exhibition game: a game played to show the public the sport. The outcome of these games is not recorded in the season's standings.

Faceoff: at the beginning of the game, two players from opposing teams crouch down with the ball on the ground between them. Both players try to scoop up the ball.

Field lacrosse: lacrosse played outdoors on a large playing field

Forward: an offensive player who carries the ball to the opposing team's net and tries to score

Mann Cup: Canada's top prize for men's Senior lacrosse

Minto Cup: Canada's top prize for men's Junior A lacrosse

Offence: a player position of someone who tries to score

Off-side: a rule that requires three players for each team to be on the offensive side of the midline, and four players on their defensive end

Penalty: when a player is removed from play for breaking a rule

Penalty box: where the player waits out a *penalty*

Playmaker: a player who figures out where to move the ball so the team can score

Playoff: game(s) played for a championship

Poke-checking: *checking* a player with the end of the stick

Power play: when one team has a player serving a penalty, the other team has an extra player on the floor

Professional: an athlete who is paid for playing a sport

Residential school: a government-run school off the reserve where Native children lived

Reserve: land owned by Natives.

Ringer: an unofficial player added to a team to help increase the chances of winning

Round robin: a tournament in which each team gets to play all the other teams

Short-handed: when a team has a player serving a penalty

Slashing: when a player hits an opposing player

with his stick

Suspend: to keep a player from playing as
    punishment for breaking rules

Titanium: a light, strong metal used to make
    lacrosse sticks

Acknowledgements

It has been a privilege and honour to write this book about Gaylord Powless. I could not have told his story without the help of his family. They generously welcomed me into their homes, shared their memories and photos of Gaylord, taught me about lacrosse and life on the reserve, read through drafts of the manuscript for accuracy, and put me in touch with people who knew Gaylord and Ross. Special thanks go to Gaylene Powless and her children Kahner and Kali, Michelle Powless-Anderson, Audrey Powless-Bomberry, Gail Ayres, Richard Powless, Tony Powless, Delby Powless Sr., Roland "Pug" Martin, and Roger "Buck" Smith.

Thank you also to Derek Drake at the Ontario Lacrosse Hall of Fame, and the staff at the Toronto Reference Library and the Woodland Cultural Centre.

The following books and publications were very helpful: *Lacrosse: A History of the Game* by Donald M. Fisher, *American Indian Lacrosse: Little Brother of War* and *Lacrosse Legends of the First Americans* by Thomas Vennum, *Lacrosse: The National Game of the Iroquois* by Diane Hoyt-Goldsmith, *Children of the Longhouse* by Joseph Bruchac, *Joseph Brant* by A. Roy Petrie, *The Man Who Ran Faster Than Everyone: The Story of Tom Longboat* by Jack Batten, *To Run with Longboat: Twelve Stories of Indian Athletes in Canada* by Brenda Zeman, *Great Athletes from Our First Nations* by Vincent Schilling, *Great Canadian Sports Stories: A Century of Competition* by Trent Frayne and Peter Gzowski, *Reserve Communities: A Six Nations History Unit* by Woodland Indian Cultural Educational Centre, and "Little Brother of War," an article by Bryan Eddington in *Beaver* magazine. I frequently referred to old issues of the *Globe and Mail*, *Toronto Star*, and *The Expositor*, and broadcasts from the CBC archives.

The following websites were helpful as well:

- www.bclacrosse.com;
- www.e-lacrosse.com;
- www.greengaels.org;
- www.iroquoisnationals.com;
- www.lacrosse.ca;
- www.lacrosse.org;
- www.nll.com (National Lacrosse League);
- www.virtualmuseum.ca (Virtual Museum of Canada).

Finally, sincere thanks to the Ontario Arts Council and the Canada Council for the Arts for supporting this project, Faye Smailes and the team at James Lorimer & Company for guiding this book to publication, Steve Sutherland (lacrosse expert, cousin, and writing buddy) for reading drafts and helping with the research, and my wonderful family for their patience while I worked day and night to meet deadlines.

About the Author

WENDY A. LEWIS is the award-winning author of *Graveyard Girl*, *Freefall*, and the Recordbooks volume *Fire on the Water: The Red-Hot Career of Superstar Rower Ned Hanlan*.

Photo Credits

We gratefully acknowledge the following sources for permission to reproduce the images within this book.

Library and Archives Canada: p 11, p 69, front cover bottom, back cover top

Ontario Lacrosse Hall of Fame: p 15, p 81, back cover middle

Powless Family collection: p 28, p 37, p 47, p 59, p 89, p 97, p 107, p 110, back cover bottom

Toronto Reference Library: p 18

Wendy A. Lewis collection: p 86

Woodland Cultural Centre: p 27, front cover top